Other Plays
BY FERNANDO ARRABAL
Published by Grove Press

Garden
of
Delights

Garden
of
Delights

a play by

FERNANDO ARRABAL

translated from the French by

HELEN GARY BISHOP and TOM BISHOP

Grove Press, Inc. New York

Garden
of
Delights

Characters

LAIS, *beautiful actress*
TELOC, *a man*
MIHARCA, *childhood friend of* LAIS
ZENON
MC'S VOICE
VOICE OF POLICEMAN
and NINE YOUNG SHEEP (EWES)

Décor

A huge space with many columns as far as the eye can see: they form a kind of labyrinth.

Every here and there, rather far apart, one can distinguish a few small balconies between columns.

A circular moving platform allows for the entrance and exit of a small green for the NINE YOUNG SHEEP. *A gate keeps them from getting out.*

Act One

Darkness.
A single spot grows brighter on LAIS *until she is*
entirely visible. The remainder of the stage remains in
the shadows. LAIS *seems to have stepped out of an old*
engraving: her arms are bare, a plunging décolletage,
a tiered gown, a rococo chapeau on her head. She sings
very sweetly and sentimentally.

LAIS (*singing*)   Such is life, seeming so delectable,
   Like a siren, affected and mutable,
   She envelops and plunges us into her sweetness,
   Until death comes to break the oar and cable,
   And of us remains but a fable,
   Less than wind, smoke, dream, and darkness.

   Or she might sing the following song.

Sadness surrounds me, mute like stupidity
I cannot even escape misunderstandings
When betrayal accuses me with its black heart
of electrolysis, of Wednesdays, and tempests.
I will speak out for a million lemons instead of for
   glory
And I feel a bubble rising into my brain
From my pained heart screaming of madness.

   Another spot suddenly lights up a corner of the
   stage where the live baby SHEEP *bleat timidly.*
   LAIS *talks to them.*

LAIS (*with love and tenderness*) Hush there, my pretty ones. I'm right here with you, you're not alone.

A few of the SHEEP *continue to bleat.*

Don't be afraid of anything. The big bad wolf doesn't exist. No one will slaughter you. Those are stories invented by men. Poor little things. (*She sings the song to herself again, then hums it softly.*) Are you calmed down now? But you must have your dinner, it's getting late. Tomorrow I'll buy you anything you want. I'll give each of you a wrist watch so you'll know exactly when I'll return. Poor little darlings, have your dinner in peace. I don't want you to have nightmares. My poor little ones, my darlings! And I'll even buy you a television set if you'd like. . . . All right now, it's dinnertime!

Suddenly a tremendous roar is heard, like the lamentation of a savage beast. LAIS *runs to turn on a light. She seems frightened. The stage lights up entirely. Above we make out a cage, and inside it the beast who roared. The cage is suspended about fifteen feet above the stage by means of a thick rope which is worked by a pully.* LAIS *grabs hold of the rope and brings the cage down. At precisely this moment the phone rings. Another roar is heard from the cage.* LAIS *hesitates: she doesn't know whether to bring the cage down entirely or answer the telephone. She decides to answer the telephone.*

LAIS Hello.

MC's VOICE Good evening, I'm the emcee of the TV show.

LAIS Oh yes.

MC's VOICE The program will begin in a few minutes. Are you ready?

LAIS Yes, I'm here.

MC's VOICE Now here's how we shall proceed: first we'll show a fast film resumé of your extraordinary acting career. I must reiterate that it will be very difficult to make our audience understand why you refused to come to the studio to tape the interview part of the show yourself. Uh, in case you've changed your mind about that I assure you that I can get a crew over to your home in a matter of minutes to tape your answers to the audience's questions, and . . .

LAIS No, please don't start that again.

MC's VOICE Very well, we'll do it your way, but I assure you the show without your presence just won't get the same ratings.

LAIS Well then, it might be better if we canceled it.

MC's VOICE No! uh no, no, I assure you, it'll work out fine. I have a tendency to exaggerate things, pay no attention to me. Well, now, as agreed, we'll phone you four or five times during the show and one member of the studio audience will ask you questions. And you will reply from the privacy of your own home.

LAIS I don't see any other way of doing it.

MC's VOICE Very well. Stand by!

A roar of impatience from the cage. LAIS *runs to the rope and brings the cage all the way down.*

5

Inside is a creature which resembles a man, but is hairy like an animal, with gestures like an ape: ZENON. He is in his natural state, half naked. Now he is groaning with pleasure. Once the cage touches the floor, LAIS opens the door. ZENON laughs and shows his teeth; he comes out of his cage, happy.

LAIS (*very tenderly*) Easy there, little boy. Give me your hand. Come out, come on. Give me your hand.

ZENON jumps all around her, happily. He makes a huge leap and tries to take her in his arms.

LAIS Be careful, you'll crush me.

He does seem to be squeezing her too strenuously. ZENON moans with happiness and jumps from one column to another. From the top of one of them he cries:

ZENON Me . . . see . . . me . . . see . . . me see you . . . you . . . p . . . pre . . . pretty.

He expresses himself with great difficulty, stutteringly. He seems to know only a few words. It is clear that he has an adoration for LAIS. She seems to have a tender affection for him.

LAIS (*very tenderly*) Now come on, get down from there. Acting like a baby at your age.

He goes on jumping from column to column. Between moments of joyful laughter, he murmurs almost unintelligibly:

6

ZENON   Very . . . very . . . pr . . . pretty . . . you . . . very . . . very . . . pre . . . pretty.

LAIS   Now calm down, come put your head in my lap, and I'll tell you the story of the princess whose heart was full of skyscrapers.

ZENON *jumps down from a column and falls upon* LAIS *as he tries to take her into his arms; instead he knocks her to the floor and hurts her.*

LAIS (*angry*)   Look what you've done! You struck me in the breast. I could get cancer. You brute! I can't let you out for two minutes. You break everything and hurt me. I should keep you locked up all day long!

ZENON *is contrite, he knows he's done something wrong, and he scratches the floor, head lowered.*

ZENON   Me . . . bad. (*He picks something up from the floor.*) Take . . . now . . . me . . . me . . . good . . . gift . . . gift . . . (*He offers* LAIS *something he holds between his huge fingers.*)

LAIS (*disgusted*)   A fly? Is that your gift?

ZENON   Fly . . . pr . . . pretty . . . (*Seeing that she won't accept it,* ZENON *examines the fly carefully and eats it with satisfaction.*)

LAIS   Don't eat that!

ZENON (*laughs*)   . . . Already . . . ate . . .

LAIS   The things you do!

The telephone rings.

(*To* ZENON)   And now you be quiet, be good, don't make any noise. Do you hear?

7

ZENON (*laughs*) Yes.

LAIS I'm not joking. While I'm on the phone, I don't want to hear a peep out of you.

ZENON (*laughs like a child*) Yes.

LAIS (*picks up the telephone*) Hello . . .

MC's VOICE This is WITI-TV calling.

LAIS Good evening.

MC's VOICE (*very sophisticated*) Lais, the greatest actress of the century and the most secretive, will reply to questions from our audience. Are you ready, Lais?

LAIS Yes.

MC's VOICE Thank you. A lovely young lady with charming pigtails will start with the first question.

VOICE OF GIRL FROM AUDIENCE I'd like to ask you, if you don't mind, how you live? Is it true, as they say, that you live alone in like a huge castle away from everybody, except for when you act?

LAIS I'm not actually alone . . .

GIRL Who do you live with?

Long silence.

LAIS Uh, well . . . (*Pause.*) With my memories, my ghosts too. I speak to them and they live with me as though they were flesh-and-blood people.

MC's VOICE Thank you very much, Lais, for your frank answer to our first question. We shall be returning to you later.

LAIS Very well.

She puts down the phone. The SHEEP *bleat in the background.*

8

My little ones, what's the matter? Haven't you had dinner yet?

> LAIS *sets the platform into motion and the sheep move onstage.*

Oh what a silly I am! You want me to feed you, don't you?

> LAIS *grabs a pitchfork and goes toward the sheep pen and their feeder. She feeds them their "dinner" with the fork and the* SHEEP *bleat with pleasure.*

How beautiful you are, my sweet ones!

> LAIS *caresses them and kisses them.* ZENON *growls furiously.*

You keep still! (*To the* SHEEP.) That's right, you eat my darlings. You are my most precious treasures. You're my warm and moving hopes and dreams.

> *Pause. Sound of hand bells. Darkness. The platform turns, the* SHEEP *disappear. Sound of hand bells.*

The light returns, very different. Onstage, MIHARCA *and* LAIS.

MIHARCA (*playing a nun*)   You are a stubborn and willful child.

LAIS (*as a young girl*) But Sister . . .

MIHARCA You are all the same and you are worse than the others. You all deserve to be whipped.

LAIS I didn't do anything.

MIHARCA What's that in your hand?

LAIS Nothing.

MIHARCA Is that so? Give it here.

LAIS No Sister, please.

MIHARCA Open up your hand, Celestine!

LAIS Sister, please . . .

> *The nun snatches the piece of paper from* LAIS' *hand savagely.* LAIS *closes her eyes tight.*

MIHARCA What does this mean? What are all these sketches? (*She reads.*) "I swear that one day I'll be free, I swear that God does not exist, I swear that my name is not Celestine but Lais, I swear . . ." You will be punished for this. Put her in the cell!

LAIS No Sister, please, not that.

MIHARCA Just look at the way you revolt against us. Such gratitude! You who have neither mother nor father. If it weren't for us you'd be a beggar girl on the streets!

> LAIS, *in the cell. She's crying. She interrupts her crying and exclaims fiercely:*

LAIS I'll show them . . . I swear that I'll be free, I swear that my name is not Celestine but Lais . . .

> *A knock is heard from the other side of the wall.*

MIHARCA'S VOICE Are you all right?

LAIS Yes.

MIHARCA's VOICE Listen, raise the loose board on your side of the wall and I'll be able to come visit you.

LAIS *raises the board and* MIHARCA *appears. She is one of* LAIS' *girlfriends.*

MIHARCA Poor little Lais, always being punished.

LAIS I'll show them, I'll show them.

MIHARCA Calm down. Here, have a drink (*She extends a drinking horn full of water.*)

LAIS The sisters hate me. No one loves me.

MIHARCA Don't say silly things. One day we'll get out of here and we'll be happy. And I love you.

LAIS When I get out of here I'll be freer than free. I'll have everything: transparent eggs full of harps and tricycles, earthworms and zebras, and I'll go out walking with them in French gardens, with a bouquet of pansies for my parasol and I'll have, I'll . . . (*Furious.*) I'll have an enormous caldron of boiling shit where I'll throw all those people who've made me suffer up to now . . .

MIHARCA I'll give you a gift of a pencil to draw all your plans with and its eraser will wipe away all your nightmares.

Pause.

Have you tried any new experiments?

LAIS Yes, look! (*Very ceremoniously.*) Look at my hand. (*In her closed hand a small intense light shines.*)

MIHARCA What's that?

LAIS I don't know. But keep looking because it'll soon disappear.

MIHARCA What a bright light! . . . Maybe it's God hiding in your hand in order to love you better.

LAIS God . . . then you think that God doesn't hate me, that He hasn't forgotten me? (*Dreamily.*) You think that God is watching me and protecting me as though I were a lost sheep in a forest of wolves?

At that moment the light disappears for good.

He's gone.

MIHARCA You're wonderful. I really do love you.

They embrace each other lovingly.

LAIS I love you too.

MIHARCA *raises her skirt abruptly and shows her buttocks.*

MIHARCA If you love me so much, kiss my ass.

LAIS Me?

She hesitates. The telephone rings. Darkness.

The action resumes in the "habitual" décor. The lights become "normal" again. The phone rings. LAIS, *adult, picks up the telephone.*

MC'S VOICE Dear Lais, whom we all admire, one of the ladies in our audience would like to ask a question. Are you ready?

LAIS Yes.

VOICE OF LADY Rumor has it that you once committed a crime. In fact I heard that it was horrible and that you . . .

MC's VOICE I have to interrupt you, Madame, and ask you not to ask questions based on malicious gossip which certain unscrupulous papers and magazines will publish merely for their sensation value.

VOICE OF LADY Oh, I'm so sorry. May I ask another question?

MC's VOICE Go ahead.

VOICE OF LADY They say that you were an orphan, is that true?

LAIS Yes, it's true.

VOICE OF LADY I can imagine how much you suffered.

LAIS I'm sorry to disappoint you, but actually my parents became a marvelous dream. I have always felt sad and sorry for all those people who have had to endure the dull reality of their real parents, most of whom are banal and boring. But I was free to imagine mine as being strange and fascinating; I could be the bastard daughter of Einstein, or the child of Neptune and a Roman slave, a creature come alive from the imaginings of a mad genius of a poet.

MC's VOICE Thank you very much, Lais, for your answer . . . (*Slightly affected tone.*) which was so . . . poetic. We'll be right back.

LAIS *puts down the telephone.*

ZENON Me . . . me . . . be . . . your pa . . . papa . . . and . . . your mama . . . (ZENON *takes her into his huge arms and rocks her like a baby. With a flashlight which he finds next to him he tries to give*

her a baby bottle.) Bo . . . bottle . . . for . . . my
. . . ba . . . baby girl . . .
LAIS (*breaking free*)   You're so stupid!
ZENON   Spank . . . for little girl . . . ba . . . bad
little . . . girl.

> *They chase each other between the columns. Dark-*
> *ness.*

Lights up, different. The nun reappears.

MIHARCA (*as nun*)   Don't think that we dislike you,
my child. God has taught us that we must love each
other and even the most depraved of creatures. One
day you will leave here since it seems that God has
not decided to call you into His service.

> LAIS, *as young girl, listens.*

We will place you in a fine home and you will be a
perfect house servant, since we have taught you how
to do everything. Now you must not forget the
prayers which every object in the home has inspired. Repeat with me.

> *They pray together.*

MIHARCA   The refrigerator.
MIHARCA *and* LAIS (*together*)   Blessed art thou for
my brother, the refrigerator, who is responsible for
conserving the fragile life of my sisters, the vita-
mins. Oh, if only I were more careful about conserving life, less impressionable to the ideas of cor-

ruption, conservative enough to cherish traditions.

MIHARCA   The thermostat.

MIHARCA *and* LAIS (*together*)   Blessed art thou for my brother the thermostat, obedient gadget of atmosphere. He suggests a humble and discreet role to me: that I maintain the tone, without subterfuge, which is required, not more not less.

We continue to hear the murmur of their prayers. LAIS runs in the countryside, flowers in her hand; she seems very happy and she rolls around on the grass. She cries out.

LAIS   May I be blessed a thousand and one times, may I have the most beautiful face in the world, may my body produce ten thousand tiny alligators, all white and shining to illuminate my happiness. May I be blessed a thousand and one times . . .

She continues to roll around and finds herself suddenly at the feet of a man (TELOC) who stands, legs apart, and laughs aloud. He holds a trumpet in his hands. LAIS tries to run away, but TELOC catches her.

TELOC   Where are you going, you who run in these woods?

LAIS   Don't tell the sisters!

TELOC *laughs.*

TELOC (*with authority*)   Sit down here at my feet. (*He laughs again.*)

LAIS   You won't tell anyone that I ran away?

15

TELOC Don't worry, little girl . . . tell me what happened.

LAIS The sisters beat me and I ran away.

TELOC Do you see those fields?

LAIS Yes.

TELOC Do you see those mountains?

LAIS Yes.

TELOC Do you see those birds flying?

LAIS Yes.

TELOC Well, you are just as free as they are. And like them your eyes sing of your love for liberty.

LAIS They do?

TELOC Yes. Now clean my shoes with your skirt, they're very dirty.

> LAIS *seems a little frightened, but she executes the order very attentively.*

Look at my chest!

LAIS It looks very strange.

TELOC My chest has hair on it and yours doesn't. (*He laughs.*)

LAIS That's not all . . . I seem to see stairs?

TELOC Oh, you saw them. Well on those stairs my thoughts climb from my heart to my head, also my desires descend from my brain to my belly.

LAIS How pretty they are! (*Silence. She looks carefully at his chest.*) And those ropes . . . and those shelves with little books . . . and those pots . . .

TELOC Be careful, they're very small.

LAIS There's one that's very shiny with a sign on it: pear jam.

TELOC (*angrily*) Don't touch that, my soul is in there.

LAIS Your soul is the pear jam?

TELOC   And yours, what is it?

LAIS   Well, I don't know. But what difference does it make? The sisters tell me that since I am bad my soul will go to Hell anyway.

TELOC   Don't believe it. (*He takes a normal-sized jar of jam out of his pocket.*) Look at this jar . . . I'll make you a gift of it and as soon as you can, put your soul in there.

LAIS   How beautiful it is! How big it is! What beautiful designs on it. How strange they are!

TELOC   You will put your soul in there.

LAIS   But I don't know whether mine is pear jam or something else.

TELOC   You should know. My soul does everything I want it to.

LAIS   Is that so?

TELOC   Absolutely.

LAIS   Let's see. (*Abruptly.*) At this very moment make a red parachute with a purple fringe fall with a crystal ball holding a goldfish with wings inside it.

TELOC   At this very moment.

The chute falls. LAIS *is stunned as she realizes that the chute has fallen as she asked.*

No need to say anything. It's perfectly normal. But since you're a very sensitive little girl, I'm going to do something very special for you . . . that other people would certainly not understand.

LAIS   What's that?

TELOC   What is your favorite tune?

LAIS   I love Schubert's "Ave Maria." The sisters taught it to me. I sing in the choir.

TELOC   Go ahead and sing it then; I'll accompany you.

17

LAIS   On the trumpet?

TELOC   The trumpet is too common . . . I'll do much better. Only you will be able to appreciate it.

> *The duo which follows should be one of great exaltation.* LAIS *sings the "Ave Maria" and* TELOC *accompanies her with his farting. He manages all the notes.*

LAIS   But . . .

TELOC   Yes, I'll accompany you with my farting.

LAIS   That's marvelous.

> LAIS *sings the "Ave Maria" and* TELOC *accompanies her. They look at each other happily, in ecstasy. Then* TELOC *plays the "Ave Maria" at a much faster pace on the trumpet, solo. We hear the music a long time. Darkness.*

> *The action continues.*

LAIS' VOICE (*adult*)   Where are my darlings?

> *Bleating of the* SHEEP. *The rotating platform brings them back.*

Don't be impatient, my pretty ones, I'm coming to see you.

> ZENON *becomes excited and growls.*

ZENON   Me . . . Me!

LAIS' VOICE   Be quiet, don't act like an animal.

ZENON   Everything for . . . sheep . . . No . . . Nothing for me . . .

> LAIS *appears. Her head is covered with electric wires.* ZENON *goes to see her.*

LAIS   Leave me alone. I'm giving myself an encephalogram.

> *We see that the wires do in fact lead to a machine.*

Help me . . . (*To the* SHEEP *as she caresses them.*) Poor little things, my darlings. Tomorrow I'll give you sardines for breakfast, you love them so. Now go to sleep for a while. (*She puffs up their pillows. She makes them disappear.*) God, I'm going mad . . . giving pillows and sardines to sheep . . . ah, why not?

> ZENON *is furious to see* LAIS *giving so much attention to the* SHEEP; *he grabs a pillow and rips it to pieces and tries to get others.*

What are you doing? Calm down.

> ZENON *is wild.*

ZENON   Everything . . . for sheep. (*He goes on tearing apart the pillows, feathers fly everywhere.*)
LAIS   Calm down or I'll lock you up in your cage.

> *His destructive rage continues.*

All right . . . it's the cage!

LAIS *threatens him with a stick.* ZENON *crouches and throws himself at her feet . . . he tries to lick them.*

I've told you not to lick my feet.

ZENON, *at her feet, seeks forgiveness.*

Well then, be good and help me. I want to know what I'm like. When I give you a sign, tell me what's showing on the encephalogram.

ZENON *goes to the machine.*

LAIS   Good. (*She gets into a chaise longue and closes her eyes.*) All right, I'm ready . . . now let's see, I'm going to think of . . . Miharca.

Long silence, she seems lost in meditation. All at once she becomes agitated, bad-tempered. ZENON *is intrigued, runs back and forth, excitedly.*

What did you see?
ZENON   Where?
LAIS   On the sheet coming out of the machine?
ZENON   Small lines . . . sma . . . small lines.
LAIS   What kind of lines, straight ones or crooked?
ZENON   Not crooked . . . str . . . straight . . . pretty . . . lines.

He jumps for joy. She goes over herself to read the sheets.

LAIS   It looks as though . . . I . . . I'm going to

think of Teloc now. (*Long silence. She meditates, seems joyous, in ecstasy, smiles.*) Teloc!

ZENON *peering at machine with attention.*

LAIS   What's happening?

ZENON   Sma . . . small lines . . . small . . .

LAIS (*tears off the electrical wire furiously*)   What the devil use is this damn machine now that I think of it? . . . I am neither going to give birth nor become Prime Minister that I know of. What difference does it make? Am I going mad or what? Tomorrow I'll hook up the sheep. (*She sobs all of a sudden.*) Lord, my God . . . I am alone on this earth . . . I'd give up everything, I'd stop acting, I'd retire. But please look my way, I, the most humble of creatures, the saddest and loneliest. I'm here doing the best I can with this life which depresses and horrifies me and for which I am not prepared. God, make me like the others so that I may find peace and resign myself to my fate. Lord, don't forget me, your most unworthy servant. Now I realize very clearly that nothing I do makes any sense, that my life is a total failure, that nothing is worth the effort, and that I have known no love for anyone. (*She cries.*) I'll put a string of thorns around my thigh, I'll wear a hair shirt and I'll do penance. And if you ask me to I'll take a teaspoon and scoop out my eye in order to offer it to you. (*She mimes this scene in so realistic a manner as to be horrible. All at once, hysterical.*) Enough! Stop! Idiot! Stupid Lais! Dumb bitch! Take out your eye! Are you crazy or what? You are a famous actress. The *best!* And God let you get born thoughtlessly, with the help of two pairs of

21

asses run through with a dart. (*To* ZENON.) Come! I'll start my life over with you, we'll get married, the two of us.

> ZENON *runs to her joyously.*

We'll get married and I'll live a normal life. We'll give dinner parties, we'll go to the races, I'll have lovers, we'll buy a TV set and a country house, we'll practice yoga and acupuncture . . . Yes, I'll open wide my door and the whole world will see how I live. My secret life is over: I have nothing more to hide. (*She screams.*) I'm so happy . . . bring the costumes, we'll get married at once.

> ZENON *goes to get costumes.*

The sheep will be our witnesses. They'll sign with a lick from their tongues.

> ZENON *returns, thrown together in what looks like a bride's gown. Upon seeing him,* LAIS *laughs, awkward, uncomfortable.*

Are you going to be the bride?
ZENON (*happily*) Yes, yes, me . . . bri . . . bride . . . you . . . husba . . . band.

> LAIS *steps into tuxedo pants which she wears over her gown and puts on a top hat. In the background we hear the* SHEEP *bleating and the wedding march. In a grotesque and yet touching manner, they walk arm in arm toward one of the columns.* ZENON *looks exactly like a gorilla covered with a*

*bridal veil. This scene should be played grandi-
osely, full of music and sounds.*

LAIS (*playing priest*)   Zenon, do you take this man
Lais as your husband, to honor and feed, to give him
your groin of flames and honey, til death do you
part?

ZENON *grunts "uh huh" happily.*

Say "yes, I swear."

The phone rings. LAIS *goes toward the phone as
she takes off her tuxedo.*

MC's VOICE   Are you ready, Lais?

LAIS   Go ahead.

MC's VOICE (*to a woman in the audience*)   You may
ask your question.

WOMAN's VOICE   First of all, I would like to tell you
that your performance in *Fando and Lis* was wonderful.

LAIS   Thank you.

WOMAN's VOICE   Although I must say I didn't like the
play at all . . . I thought it didn't make much sense,
it was cold, and much too close to *Romeo and Juliet,*
which inspired it.

MC's VOICE   Please, Madame, we are not here to do
theater criticism.

WOMAN's VOICE   But in that play you were a woman
in love, and very convincingly. Have you ever been
in love?

LAIS   There have been . . . men.

WOMAN's VOICE   I've heard that during your adolescence, while you were still with the sisters . . . a man uh . . . and uh that he disappeared forever afterward.

LAIS He . . . he was . . . an exceptional person, blessed with many magic powers I never understood . . . I'll make the usual statement: everything I know, even in the theater, is thanks to him.

MC's VOICE Thank you very much for your reply, which I am sure has satisfied the lady.

WOMAN's VOICE I'd like to know . . .

They are cut off. LAIS *remains pensive a few moments, then exits.*

The lights change.

LAIS (*offstage, as young girl*) Miharca! Miharca!

Silence.

Miharca! Miharca!

MIHARCA *as young girl appears, then* LAIS.

LAIS We've got to get out of here.

MIHARCA What for? The sisters love us, we're together, we're happy.

LAIS Let's do something; travel around the world, be free . . . let's do it now!

MIHARCA What's the matter with you?

LAIS Come with me. You're the only one who really understands me . . . here . . .

MIHARCA What do you mean *here?*

LAIS Well . . . uh . . . here.

MIHARCA You know someone on the outside?

LAIS You won't tell?

MIHARCA No, promise.

LAIS I met a man, a beautiful person . . . with stairs on his chest and his soul in a jar of jam . . .

MIHARCA You're crazy.

LAIS Come with me, you'll see.

They run together in and out of the archways between the columns, giggling and squealing like two mischievous little girls.

LAIS Teloc! Teloc!

No one appears.

Teloc! Teloc!

Still no one.

MIHARCA You see! You made it up, there's no one.

LAIS No, there is . . . *Teloc!*

MIHARCA You made me sneak out of school, take a chance on getting punished, for nothing.

LAIS Well then, let's run away for good, now.

MIHARCA No, we can't.

LAIS Let's do it, let's escape.

MIHARCA Don't leave me.

LAIS (*change of mood, euphoria subsiding*) Then Teloc isn't real . . . he doesn't exist . . . oh, I feel sick. I'm afraid . . . do you think I'm going to die?

MIHARCA Don't be silly!

LAIS But I feel like I'm going to die . . . oh, I don't

25

want to die, even if I have to go on being a rotten apple all my life, I don't want to die.

MIHARCA You won't, don't worry. We'll always be together. We'll play all our games and have fun. (MIHARCA *mimes playing a flute for* LAIS.)

LAIS I don't want to play games. I want to crawl into a cage with a flower pot and you'll come to water us both every day.

MIHARCA Look! The lions!

MIHARCA *mimes snapping a whip, lions roaring, but* LAIS *won't play.*

LAIS Miharca, do you think we're like Adam and Eve in Paradise or Botticelli's virgins? I want to spend my life with a dove sitting on top of my head and a gossamer scarf flowing around my neck.

MIHARCA (*playing*) I'm going to give you an injection.

LAIS No!

MIHARCA Lift your skirt and take down your pants. I'm going to vaccinate you against the evil eye.

LAIS No, I don't want to.

MIHARCA You see how you treat me! I do everything for you and you don't even care. I hate you. Goodby! (*She runs away.*)

LAIS Miharca! Miharca!

LAIS *cries alone. Enter* TELOC, *clothed half as a football player, half as a lumberjack.*

TELOC Little girl with little faith.

LAIS (*delighted*) Oh you *were* here. I was sure you were.

LAIS *rushes to* TELOC *and tries to clean his shoes with her skirt.*

TELOC   Don't touch me!

LAIS (*intimidated*)   I wanted my friend Miharca to meet you. We sneaked out of school to see you.

TELOC   Tell me what you would like most to do now?

LAIS   Oh I'm so happy . . . tie me to a tree and make me afraid.

TELOC   How about if we played football?

They jump around and play. They grapple for the ball on the ground. TELOC *jumps* LAIS *and pins her down.*

LAIS   Uhhh you're so heavy . . . I can't breathe.

TELOC   Poor little thing . . .

LAIS   You're hurting me with your helmet.

TELOC   Ah, my helmet is magical.

LAIS (*fascinated*)   How?

TELOC   With *this* I can travel into the past and into the future.

LAIS   Oh, I want to travel.

TELOC   Where would you like to go?

LAIS   Into the future *and* the past too. I want to see Cleopatra, Christ with Mary Magdalene. I want to see Breughel, I want to see the astronauts a thousand years from now, I want to see Buddha, Bosch . . .

TELOC   Ha, ha, ha, you'll see them all. But first, tell me how many doves there are in one wish?

LAIS (*thinks*)   Seven and eleven. But in my wish right now there's only room for you.

TELOC Well, since you're good at guessing, you might go very far. You'll be an actress.

LAIS (*wonderment*) An actress?

TELOC Wouldn't you like that?

LAIS (*quickly*) Oh yes, I'd love to be an actress only I have a bad memory . . . and I'd be ashamed to show my legs . . .

TELOC You'd do as you liked about that.

LAIS (*relieved*) Oh really?

TELOC Would you be so ashamed to show your legs?

LAIS Yes, very. The sisters told me that God sees all the bad things we do and that we should never take all our clothes off, not even to go to bed. When we take a bath, we wear a long nightshirt slit up the side so we can soap ourselves without being . . . naked.

TELOC Show me your legs.

LAIS My legs?

TELOC Right up to the thighs.

LAIS (*shocked*) The thighs . . . but it's a sin.

TELOC Forget it!

LAIS No, I'll do it . . . for you. (*Raising her skirt slightly.*) Is that enough?

TELOC I can't even see your knees.

LAIS But if I raise it higher . . .

TELOC (*angry*) Never mind.

LAIS Don't be angry.

TELOC I'm not angry.

LAIS You looked as if you were.

TELOC All I know is that if you really trusted me . . .

LAIS I do . . . look. (*She raises her skirt quickly and uncovers her thighs for a moment.*)

TELOC But I didn't see anything.

LAIS I have to show them longer?

28

TELOC   Of course. I want to *see* your thighs.

LAIS   Oh, that's really bad.

TELOC   You must close your eyes and show me your thighs until I say "enough."

LAIS   . . . All right, but afterward I'll have to go to Confession. I'll say it was windy and . . . no, I mustn't lie . . . oh, here goes.

Resigned and resolved like a person taking a plunge, she shows her thighs for a good while. TELOC *comes close to her, and with a colored crayon writes the word "hope" on her thighs. "Ho" on one side and "pe" on the other.*

TELOC   Enough. Open your eyes and let down your skirt.

LAIS   What did you do?

TELOC   I wrote on you.

LAIS   Oh, write some more, that felt nice.

TELOC   Quiet! We're going to go on a trip through time.

LAIS   You said I would be an actress.

TELOC   You will be an actress; the reincarnation of God on earth. You will be the Messiah; you will assume all the worries and wonders of the whole world. You will be beaten, tortured, loved . . . and then you'll remove your mask, just like in real life.

LAIS   Oh please, the tortures right away.

TELOC   What kind do you like?

LAIS   I don't know.

TELOC   You'd better decide.

LAIS   You know, there are times when I become very devout and I really believe in God and I speak to him and I put on a hair shirt in the morning, and I

29

go from the dormitory to the church with my hair
shirt and a string of thorns around my thigh, and
I feel great pain and during Mass I understand that
I am doing it for God and God smiles at me, and I
can feel him right there in my thigh; I feel that He
thanks me and that He and I will be friends forever.
And when Mass is over, I rush back to the dormitory for the most painful, the most beautiful moment of all, when I take off my hair shirt and undo
the string of thorns. My thigh is all swollen and
when I pull out the tiny thorns which stick in my
flesh, the blood spurts out and I feel great pain and
pleasure at the same time and I know that God is
all around me and I feel him taking me into his arms
and once I'm there, warm and safe, I can cry without
being afraid of Hell or Purgatory or any of the thousands of punishments I'll receive for my countless
sins and because I ran away from school and talked
back to the sisters and because I hate them even
though they took me in when my parents didn't want
me and had left me an orphan . . .

TELOC   Oh stop that drivel, you stupid girl.

LAIS (*hurt*)   You're making fun of me.

TELOC   I don't want you leafing through your dreary
family album in my presence.

LAIS   Then tell me, what kind of an actress shall I be?

TELOC   Didn't you want to go on a trip?

LAIS   Oh yes, I still do.

TELOC   Well then, put on the helmet.

LAIS   Tell me, will I sing, will I dance?

TELOC   No, you'll be an actress.

LAIS   Will you let me do a dance just for you?

TELOC   Do you know how to dance?

LAIS   I dance sometimes when I'm by myself, and

sometimes I sing too. I make believe I'm in a palace ballroom . . . like this. (LAIS *goes through a frantic dance, very different from any kind of real dancing. She does a sort of hysterical, convulsive movement. At first she moves about a great deal; then she slows down. With deliberate innocence she rubs her belly with her hands, throws herself back like a mad creature. All of this seems insane and hysterical. She ends up, rear up, head down.*)

TELOC   So that's your dance?

LAIS   Yes, now come dance with me.

TELOC   No, singing the other day was enough. I'm no good at acrobatics.

LAIS   Oh, our song was so beautiful. Do you know I haven't told anyone about it, not even Miharca?

TELOC   Very good. For that you get a kiss on the forehead. (*He kisses her forehead.*)

LAIS   More!

TELOC   What a little glutton you are.

LAIS   Look, I'm putting on the helmet. (*She does.*)

TELOC   And you will start your trip in time.

LAIS   Oh, oh, oh, my head's spinning. Oh!

A kind of cone of transparent light falls on LAIS. *Vague images begin to become distinguishable. They flash on a sort of screen which has just fallen between two columns.*

TELOC's VOICE   Press the buttons on the helmet and you'll be able to go into the future and the past.

LAIS *presses the buttons. Like a magic lantern, a series of projections flash on and off as* LAIS *presses on. The stage is bathed in a strange at-*

mosphere created by real fireworks. Strange music over a background of boots, explosions, bombs, etc. Suddenly the following images appear on the screen: Superman running with girlfriend in arms. Goya's dog. A battleground from World War II, devastation. A giant Alice in Wonderland. The professor and the nightclub singer, Blue Angel. Hundred Years War, devastation. Two lovers of Chagall. An advertising poster. The painting "The Birth of Arrabal." The painting "The Garden of Delights" by Bosch. The same images come on again at a dizzying speed until LAIS *rips off the helmet. Everything returns to normal.*

LAIS   I don't know how to use it. Everything went too fast.

TELOC   With these buttons you go forward or backward.

LAIS   I'm so afraid. It's awful . . . war is awful.

TELOC   You have to learn to use it. The red button goes into the past and the little needle shows you the place and the century. If you want the future, it's the black button. You were making the needle jump in all directions.

LAIS   I didn't know . . . but I don't want to see the past, I'm too afraid.

TELOC   Why?

LAIS   There are so many dead, so many wars, so much suffering.

TELOC   Weren't you asking for torture a while ago?

LAIS   But that was different. If you torture me, it's because you love me. When you're close to me I can feel how alive you are, and . . .

TELOC All right, let's throw the helmet away then.

LAIS No! Please, I'd like to see more. I'd like to watch some of the ceremonies of my life . . . like my first Communion . . . and those to come . . . my wedding . . . my death.

Phone rings. Darkness.

The phone rings. The action resumes. The lights become "normal." The stage is empty: in a corner, the phone rings. ZENON *enters, he tries to pick up the receiver. He grabs the phone books and tears out pages as he laughs. The* SHEEP *bleat: they have just reappeared. The phone keeps ringing insistently and* ZENON, *more and more frenetic, continues to rip pages out of the phone books. Bleating of* SHEEP.

LAIS' VOICE (*adult*) Hush there, my poor little things, this evening I shall read you the story of *Alice*. But right now be quiet; they're phoning me again.

The SHEEP *bleat.* LAIS *enters.*

LAIS Look what you've done, you beast. (*She seems very nervous; she would like to pick up the ringing phone, but at the same time wants to scold* ZENON, *tie him up, and keep him quiet.*) I can't leave you out two minutes before you start doing something stupid, you break everything, you tear my clothes, rip up my shoes, and now my phone books. (*She is on the verge of tears.*) God, what have I done to deserve such punishment, why must I be deprived of any happiness or peace? And now you be quiet!

I'm going to tie you up so you'll quiet down. And if you go on jumping around I'll put you in your cage and you'll stay there all night long.

ZENON *drops his head; he seems to be very sorry.*

ZENON Me . . . bad . . . me . . . love you. (*He tries to kiss her, to put his arms around her.*)

LAIS Stop that and be still. You can hear the phone, can't you? Leave me alone, I'll send you to a zoo, to the pound, to an institution. I don't see why I have to go on sacrificing my life for you.

She ties him to a column. ZENON *tries to kiss her.*

And now keep still and be quiet!

The phone has gone on ringing. She finally picks it up.

MC's VOICE Here we are back again with you, Lais, I hope we're not disturbing you.

LAIS No, no, not at all.

MC's VOICE Another lady from our audience would like to ask a question.

LAIS Go right ahead.

LADY's VOICE I think you are the most beautiful woman I have ever seen.

LAIS Don't say things like that. There are many beautiful women and I . . .

LADY's VOICE Well, then how does it affect you to know that you are one of the most beautiful?

LAIS I never found myself beautiful, on the contrary, when I was little I thought myself ugly. The, uh, place where I spent my youth, the people who raised me, told me I wasn't pretty. And for many years I really believed I was one of the most repugnant beings on earth. I was sure that I would never be able to have . . . a lover . . . and that if one day I wanted to become a woman, I would only be able to do it with some sort of monster or an exceptionally ugly man whom I would pay for his services. For a long time . . . (*She hesitates.*)

At that very instant, we hear ZENON *say very distinctly as he takes advantage of the silence and with unusually good elocution:*

ZENON   I want to . . . bugger you.

LAIS *cups the receiver with her hand and angrily orders* ZENON *to shut up, and in a stage whisper says:*

LAIS   You'll pay for that!

MC'S VOICE   Is anything wrong, are you not feeling well . . . ?

LAIS   No, it's all right . . . I was saying . . . uh.

MC'S VOICE   Oh, your reply was more than adequate. Isn't that right?

LADY'S VOICE   Yes, thank you so much and I want you to know I'll always admire you.

LAIS *puts down the phone. She storms over to* ZENON, *near tears.*

LAIS   Do you realize what you've done? What are they going to think of me? Oh my God, what humiliation!

What torture! But why me, why, God, why! (*She takes hold of* ZENON *and makes him get into his cage and pulls the pully till he has ascended, at stage center.*) And I'll never take you out of there, you'll stay locked up forever, I'll forget all about you. You are a monster. You're determined to destroy me.

ZENON Me . . . love . . . you.

LAIS Leave me alone with your stupid declarations. If you loved me, if you really loved me . . .

ZENON *cries like a baby with loud sniffling sobs.*

That's right, go ahead and cry, cry! I'm the one who should be sobbing. I've got a right to cry. My life is hell because of you! From now on I can only trust my sheep.

The SHEEP *bleat.* LAIS *goes to them. She disappears from the view of the audience.*

LAIS' VOICE My poor little darlings, I love only you, my sweet ones. You alone are good to me. You never say a thing. I'll always love you. I'm going to write a hundred sonnets for you and I'll read them to you before I go to sleep. Come here, I have a kiss for each of you.

We hear the kissing. Darkness.

"Different" lights up. MIHARCA (*as young girl*) *enters.*

MIHARCA Lais! Lais! Where are you hiding? What are you doing, Lais? (MIHARCA *disappears.*)

We hear a prayer being murmured. It sounds like
LAIS *praying. As a light comes up on her we see
her in a kneeling position. Actually what we see
is an almost life-sized Frankenstein standing before her, which turns out to be a dummy. As the
light concentrates on them,* LAIS *stands up. She
places candles all around the Frankenstein and
lights them all with great ceremony.*

LAIS (*as young girl, to Frankenstein*) And I know
that you understand me and love me truly even
though I am ugly . . . I know that you would never
feel the disgust I would surely inspire in other men.
We shall be secretly engaged. And one day, if you
still haven't found me repulsive, you'll let me become
your wife: to make love to you. You know that I'm
very ugly and disgusting. That is I go to the toilet
at least once every day and that's very disgusting I
know and I'm very ashamed of it. I think that's the
main reason other men don't want to have anything
to do with me . . . And then, once a month . . .
and sometimes I even have bad breath too, oh nobody says anything about it, not my friends or the
sisters, so as not to hurt my feelings, but I'm sure I
smell exactly like Mother Catherine. I don't notice
it myself, of course, but that's because day and night
I'm so used to my own mouth's smell. And then I
have an awful body, misshapen. My bones stick out
all over instead of being covered with smooth, soft
flesh which I know is so attractive . . . and I don't
think my nose is well shaped either. I guess when
people see me they must say "What a catastrophe,
what a nose, all crooked," and I feel so ashamed
and I don't know where to run and hide. But I know

that you understand and love me despite my monstrous appearance. Every now and then I remind myself that I must remain a worthy fiancée for my Frankenstein and so I let a week or two pass without even washing my hands. And I end up with my nails black and my face full of dirt and I take such pleasure in thinking of you and how much you'd love me that way.

MIHARCA's VOICE   Open up!

LAIS *opens after having blown out the candles and covered her Frankenstein with a sheet.*

MIHARCA   Why did you lock yourself in?

LAIS   I was just . . . uh . . .

MIHARCA   Do you know that I dreamed of you?

LAIS   You did?

MIHARCA   I dreamed that you killed me, but after I was dead I came back to see you and you gave me a piece of white bread.

LAIS   How could you dream of something like that?

MIHARCA   It was awful to see myself dead and eating your white bread. It was really awful.

LAIS   But why did I kill you?

MIHARCA   You killed me in order to win, to enter into the garden of delights . . . It was sacrificial. . . . Swear that you don't hate me.

LAIS   Me hate you?

The bells ring.

Listen, it's bedtime.

MIHARCA   Let's go then.

LAIS   No, stay.

MIHARCA   But it's forbidden.

LAIS   So what, let's pretend we're already free.

MIHARCA   Let's play a game.

LAIS   All right, which one?

MIHARCA   I'd like to play the part of chaste St. Joseph and you can be Jesus.

LAIS   That will be difficult.

MIHARCA   Lie down, I'm going to rock you. My poor little cherished son who is going to save the world through his sufferings, with those huge nails in his hands . . .

LAIS   But I shall accomplish miracles, I'll make paralytics walk and the blind see.

MIHARCA   Now that you will become a man, look what I have brought you. (MIHARCA *takes out a huge knife with a shining blade.*) Now lie down.

LAIS   That frightens me.

MIHARCA   Never mind, just lie down.

LAIS *lies down on the floor with great apprehension.* MIHARCA *kisses the tips of* LAIS' *fingers, her forehead, and her feet.*

LAIS   What are you doing?

MIHARCA   Keep still, it's a rite. (MIHARCA *proceeds as if with a ceremony; she raises the knife high.*) Now you must scream very loud.

LAIS *screams without conviction.*

Louder!

LAIS *screams with all her might as* MIHARCA *pretends to stab her in the lower abdomen.*

That's good, look at that. (MIHARCA *proudly shows off a tiny bit of something which shines.*)

LAIS   What did you do?

MIHARCA   I circumcised you.

Cannon shots ring out. Then violin music. Darkness.

The scene changes to a prison. The shadows of bars are projected across the stage. We hear LAIS *crying. She is alone on the stage.*

LAIS (*murmuring*)   I don't want to live in a prison. I want to get out of here. What have I done? Why must I stay here day and night with that electric-light bulb staring at me constantly? Poor Lais, poor miserable Lais. (*She screams.*) I want to be free. (*After a moment.*) I'm locked in a prison in secret, nobody knows or cares, I've been forgotten, I have only one visit a day from the guards who bring me water, bread, and soup. (*After a moment, with joy.*) What's that? (*She picks something up off the floor with great excitement.*) A bug. A ladybug! You'll be my friend? Oh, I'm so happy. Look how big my cell is for you. But it's all yours. You're all dusty. No matter, when they bring my soup I'll pick out a piece of lard and when its dry I'll rub you with it and you'll get all shiny. You will be the most beautiful ladybug in the world. You can be proud of that. You see I can only take three steps in one direction and three in the other. But you can do long-distance running if you like. And I could even tie a string around one of your legs and you could slip under the door and explore the surroundings . . . that way you can let me know what's happening in the corridors. And when the guard comes around at night and tosses a pail of water into my cell to keep me from sleeping, you and I will climb up on the toilet seat and stay there, huddled together, until the water evaporates. We'll have good times together, you'll see. And when I cry, don't worry, it won't be because of you, it'll be because I'm so unhappy. And when I start screaming and I look like I'm getting desperate, will you just whisper something in my ear to cheer me up? Because those are the times I want to kill myself by drinking my urine or banging my head against the bars until it bursts.

Cannon shots and violin strains.

Lights change.

LAIS (*young girl*) Teloc! Teloc!

TELOC Calm down. Calm down. I'm here waiting for you.

LAIS Make me an actress! Please make me an actress! I want to be the most beautiful woman in the world. I want to be a success, not stay the little orphan the sisters punish and whose heart is turning black and blue.

TELOC And why an actress?

LAIS Because . . . I don't know why . . . because I want to live a thousand lives I've never had, to be tall, beautiful, feminine or small, homely, and adorable, or to be able to climb a trapeze. And to know that even though I'm just me I can become all the

41

others and that gives me the power to make all the heroines of the world more human and transform myself into an ever-changing kaleidoscope.

TELOC   Did you know that objects can speak! (*Pause.*) world.

LAIS   Well then, I want to see the evening of my greatest triumph. Make me see it. Put the helmet on my head and make me see it!

TELOC   Did you know that objects can speak! (*Time.*) Why know the future? Let surprise overcome you with its stones and storms.

LAIS   No, no. Let me wear the helmet, I want to see the evening of my consecration.

TELOC   You can ask the different objects and they will answer you, it's simpler.

LAIS   No, the helmet please.

TELOC   All right . . . Look there. . . . See that boat in the marshes?

LAIS   Yes, yes, I see it.

TELOC   Did you see its unmanned oars and its lonely appearance?

LAIS   Yes, yes. But give me the helmet.

TELOC   The boat carries death, you can speak to it and ask it anything you'd like.

LAIS   I don't want to die, I want to be free and live forever and ever.

TELOC   And the river? And the street? Don't you want to speak to them?

LAIS   Give me the helmet.

TELOC *obeys. Darkness. Lights up with special effect.*

Atmosphere is particularly ominous. Bouquets drop from above stage. They are upside down and the ribbons surrounding them drift in the air. They bear LAIS' *name. Everything has a gloomy air. The feeling is lugubrious.*

VOICE Lais, believe me, I'm an experienced producer, I know what I'm talking about. During all my years in the business I've never seen such a smashing success. You were simply divine. No one can come close to you, you'll have the critics at your feet. Every celebrity who came to see you will be praising you to the skies. I heard the best of them ecstatic about you, there was just one word on their tongues: "genius." You're on the top, my girl, the top.

LAIS' VOICE Thank you, thank you.

VOICE Don't thank me. It is I who thank you in the name of acting. Good night and sweet dreams.

The door slams. LAIS *enters and walks back and forth stage center, looking happy and excited. Then she sees the flowers and is frightened. Suddenly she stops in front of the mirror and examines herself suspiciously. She makes horrible grimaces and contorts her face. Finally she slaps herself soundly.*

LAIS Who do you think you're kidding, you cheap bitch. You really fooled them all, didn't you, you phony. (*Change of tone.*) As of tomorrow I will give up the theater and I'll go far away. I'll go hunting in the virgin forest and I'll live alone with the beasts. (*She dons a safari hat and wraps a boa around her neck. She grabs a hunting rifle and appraises the outfit in her mirror. She assumes a very military pose.*) That's it, I'll be an explorer. I'll talk to the ani-

43

mals. I'll flatten my breasts, I'll wear a loincloth and I'll swing from vine to vine screaming: ah ha, ah ha, I'm Tarzan! (*She mimes this scene.*) I'll discover existentialism . . . (*Suddenly frightened she turns quickly and discovers something among some flowers: a catafalque on which lies the bust of a woman and a bit further, the legs [upside down] in a vertical position.*) Miharca, Miharca. . . . Are you dead? And your eyes? Who did that? Who could have murdered you so viciously? Miharca. It's me, Lais. . . . It's not possible. (LAIS *runs aimlessly around the room.*)

Cannon shots. Violin music. Darkness. Projections appear on screen. Breughel painting. Bosch painting. Goya painting. Prison bars. Pictures of destroyed cities. Men imprisoned. Starving children. Planes bombing. Breughel painting. Bosch painting. Goya painting. Prison bars.

Darkness. Cannon shots, Violin music. Silence. LAIS *tries to tear off the mask. She sobs.*

TELOC   What's happening?

LAIS (*young girl*)   It's not true.

TELOC   What did you see?

LAIS   Death. . . . It was a nightmare.

TELOC   My poor little Lais.

LAIS   Do you love me?

TELOC   I hate you with all my might.

LAIS   How it thrills me to hear you say it that way. I could never love anyone else but you.

TELOC   Go away!

LAIS   You're chasing me away . . . away from you?

TELOC   You've got to get used to living without me.

LAIS   I prefer to die.

TELOC   Run toward your triumph. Go on, get out!

LAIS   Put me in the pocket of your trousers, let me sit there with your change and when you buy your evening paper, you can pay for it with me.

Darkness. The action follows its "course." Lighting "normal." ZENON, *locked in his cage, suspended above stage, is restless with impatience.*

ZENON   Lais . . . let . . . me . . . ou . . . out.

   LAIS *takes off her shoes with great care.*

Loo . . . look at mm . . . me!

   Without looking at him, LAIS *sings her song softly.*

LAIS! (ZENON *roars.*)

   LAIS *is wearing a vaporous gown of tulle and over it she wears a waist-pincher.* LAIS *joins her hands together and sings her song with great feeling; she seems to be floating on air.*

ZENON   Come . . . let . . . me . . . out!

LAIS   You were bad.

ZENON   Me . . . me . . . not bad . . . me . . . love you.

   LAIS *goes on singing as though she hadn't noticed him.*

Let . . . me . . . down!

LAIS Now I love only the sheep, I'm singing for them,
I'm leaving them all my money in my will and nothing to you, and they'll get all the royalties from my
records, my photos . . .

ZENON Sheep . . . mean . . . me . . . hate.

LAIS The sheep are very sweet, they're always quiet.
Soon they will be able to speak as you do, on some
I'll put wings so that they can fly around the house
and on the others I'll put fins so that they can become sheep-sharks and be the envy of all.

ZENON Me . . . better.

LAIS You . . . terrible.

ZENON You . . . hate me . . . love . . . only sheep.

LAIS And I'll buy them each a chateau so they can
contemplate the countryside from their terraces.
And those who get sick I'll send to the hospital in a
city with canals so that they can get well while
bathing with the storks. And for you, nothing! And
when I sing, it's for them.

ZENON Sing for . . . me.

LAIS No, just for them.

ZENON They . . . not listening.

LAIS Yes they are . . . (*She sings for the sheep.*)
And I'll buy each of them sunglasses and a tanned
boyfriend, at night they'll sleep in a bed and their
little heads will rest on pillows and they'll have sweet
dreams!

ZENON Sheep . . . bad . . . sheep . . . bitches!

LAIS I won't allow you to insult them. Poor little
things. (LAIS *sings for sheep.*)

ZENON Sheep . . . not listening.

LAIS Yes, they are.

ZENON   Let me . . . squeeze . . . your nose.

LAIS   All you ever want to do is hurt me.

ZENON   A little bit . . . squeeze . . . nose . . . little squeeze . . . no blood.

LAIS   There, you see. I did well to lock you up.

ZENON *throws down a rope from his cage.*

What is that?

ZENON   You tie . . . rope to your foot . . . me . . . can touch you . . . when . . . rope touch . . . you.

LAIS   You're bad!

ZENON   Say . . . you love . . . me . . . mm . . . more than . . . sh . . . sheep.

LAIS   No!

ZENON   Say you . . . love me . . . more than . . . friend . . . you killed . . .

LAIS   Who told you that? (*Beside herself.*) I hate you with all my heart. I'll never let you out of that cage. (LAIS *raises the cage even higher.*) I thought that with you at least I'd have peace and you . . . you too! What's gotten into you? You're a monster. Tell me, have you ever gone out? Have the neighbors talked to you?

ZENON (*speaking very clearly*)   I killed . . . sheep.

LAIS   You killed my sheep? My sweet darlings, my angels, where are you? It's me, it's all right. (*She runs around stage looking for them, calling. She leaves the stage.*)

LAIS' VOICE   My sheep, my darlings.

Long silence. We hear a moan, a sound of pain. Then a scream.

47

You killed all nine of them! You cut their throats.
Oh my helpless creatures.

> *We hear nothing.* LAIS *returns to the stage holding
> one of the dead* SHEEP. *She kneels down with the
> sheep stage center directly under* ZENON's *cage.
> She seems to be silently sobbing, her face next to
> the sheep's body. We hear her intermittent sobbing
> and moaning.*

ZENON   Now . . . everything . . . for me.

> LAIS *continues to cry.*

Cry for . . . me . . .

> LAIS *moans. She is still in the same position next
> to the* SHEEP. *Suddenly something liquid falls from
> the cage.*

LAIS   What are you throwing down?
ZENON   Good . . . that good . . . pay attention . . .
to me . . . speak to . . . me!

> *She remains next to the* SHEEP. *The liquid con-
> tinues to fall a drop at a time.*

LAIS   What are you doing?
ZENON   To . . . get your . . . a . . . attention . . . to
me . . . I . . . sh . . . shit on . . . you.

> LAIS *looks up with hate on her face. The curtain
> closes quickly. We hear a hysterical scream.*

Act Two

As the curtain goes up, LAIS *is on stage and as in the first act, she is singing romantically.* ZENON *accompanies her with sounds, obviously happy, but we do not see him. The song goes softly on. We continue to hear* ZENON's *sounds on stage: we see only* LAIS *who is lit with a spot. When her song is finished, she jumps with joy. Then we realize that* ZENON, *in a kneeling position, was acting as a chair for* LAIS. *The stage lights up. We seen nine trays standing at different heights, each carrying a skeleton of a* SHEEP. *Pieces of fur remain hanging from the skeletons on three of them; the skin looks rotted.*

LAIS (*following* ZENON, *looking happy*) Even though you killed my beloved sheep, I love you, Zenon.

> ZENON *runs around happily; he climbs the columns and hangs from one of them by his feet, his head down. He puts his arms out to* LAIS *and embraces her in that position. Then he claps his hands in satisfaction.*

ZENON Egg! Egg!

> *He and* LAIS *run around the stage in loving abandon.*

LAIS You are my earthworm of happiness, my treasure trove of filth and buttercups, my own heart of hatchets.

ZENON I love y . . . you, love you.

> *They continue to cavort. This morbid love scene should become like a hallucination of frenzied joy.* ZENON *carries a huge egg on stage. Its top is cut open and it is covered with drawings by Bosch.*

LAIS No one knows that you are superior to all the men on earth and that you alone can raise me to the skies with your hands like royal eagles and giant sharks.

ZENON Egg! Egg!

> *They run all around the stage.* ZENON *brings the egg. They both play with it, turning it, clumsily, running around it. Suddenly* LAIS *stops her mad dashing; she stands still stage center, her hands joined, in an attitude of prayer.* ZENON *watches her.*

LAIS Did you know, Zenon? . . . I prayed for you, I prayed to God for you.

ZENON (*laughing*) You . . . don't believe . . . in God.

LAIS That's true, but just the same I prayed to God for you, for you to be happy, even if I have to suffer for you, to see that you have everything you need. Prayed for you to be saved at the hour of your death and for you to go to Heaven. God and paradise must exist, they have to exist for you who are so good.

50

While she makes this speech, ZENON *raises her skirt solemnly and kisses her knees.*

ZENON Egg! Egg!

They start chasing each other again; ZENON *finally catches* LAIS *and drags her around by her hair.*

LAIS Zenon, you're really *hurting* me.

ZENON *laughs and continues to pull* LAIS *until he has gotten her inside the egg. They are both in it and we cannot see what goes on.*

While they remain inside a kind of lovers' ritual takes place. Flowers float down around the egg. Music. A character out of Breughel crosses the stage from right to left. It is an invalid with a limp. One of his legs, bent at the knee, seems to be held tightly by a vice to which is tied a strange splint. He pulls a rowboat which is on wheels: from the boat grows a tree without leaves or flowers but on its naked branches sits a motionless black bird. A padlock is on its beak. The stage is lighted normally and remains silent for a moment. But then we hear the phone ring. It rings insistently for a long time. LAIS *comes out of the egg. She pushes it until it disappears into the wings.*

LAIS Hello.

VOICE OF POLICEMAN This is the police. You know a woman named Miharca?

51

LAIS   Yes, of course.

VOICE OF POLICEMAN   We understand you were raised in an orphanage together.

LAIS   Yes.

VOICE OF POLICEMAN   Then you haven't seen each other in a long time?

LAIS   Yes, it's been a long time, very long, but . . .

VOICE OF POLICEMAN   But what . . . ?

Silence.

Weren't you about to say something?

LAIS   No.

VOICE OF POLICEMAN   I had the feeling you were going to say you had seen her more recently.

LAIS   Yes . . . I . . .

Silence.

I saw her last night about an hour before leaving for the theater . . .

VOICE OF POLICEMAN   Yes, allow me to congratulate you, your opening was a smash hit. We heard about it at the station. They say you are the greatest actress who ever lived.

LAIS   (*interrupting him*) They came to see me here . . .

VOICE OF POLICEMAN   They? Who's they?

LAIS   She came with Teloc.

VOICE OF POLICEMAN   Teloc?

LAIS   A man we met when we were girls at the orphanage.

VOICE OF POLICEMAN   Didn't you live in?

LAIS   Yes, but we used to sneak out to see him . . . you know how girls in a boarding school are.

VOICE OF POLICEMAN   You never saw him again?

LAIS   No, never, until last night when I heard his trumpet as I was dressing to go to the theater. His trumpet . . . he was playing it in such a strange way.

A lighting effect changes the scene.

The action "resumes" the evening before.
Suddenly we hear trumpet playing. LAIS *runs on stage and dashes about looking for the player, she is half-dressed in her stage costume, which is very baroque. She seems very excited and happy at the prospect of finding* TELOC. *From a back lamp projection the enormous shadow of* TELOC *looms across the stage. At that point* LAIS *stops dashing and we find her on a small balcony on the second floor. From that vantage point she examines the trumpeter. She begins to sing the song of the first act but now she screams out the words hysterically. Alternate projections of the Bosch "Garden of Delights" and cartoon strips of today.*

LAIS   I'm here, alone like a sunflower in smoke deep in my nightmares of butterscotch and bolts.

TELOC   Where do you find the heart and the pulse?

Slowly the lights return. TELOC *is holding his trumpet in his hand.* LAIS *is wearing the same stage costume.*

53

LAIS   I'm here, huddled in a cage, between the bars of the night and crinoline petticoats.

TELOC   Poor Lais. You're alone and I can't see you or help you. Everyone makes fun of you, criticizes you, and I too abandon you. You are ridiculed and we would have all preferred that you embrace your punishment without any final fanfare.

LAIS   May I cry?

TELOC   Cry, cry to the sea and the night. But don't forget that you're wearing your finery, that you're in your stage costume and that . . .

LAIS   I can't cry. I want neither the trunk nor the rubbish. From my enchained body my soul goes out to you.

TELOC   How long has it been since we've seen each other?

LAIS   So many years! Do you remember when you showed me the stairs on your chest, and remember when you made me travel in the future and the past . . . and afterward in my bed, I'd become as tiny as solitude itself and I'd walk across the thousand and one steps of your body kissing each. Let me kiss your chest.

TELOC   No, Lais. (*He takes off his jacket and hangs it on a hook.*)

LAIS *throws herself at the jacket and kisses it passionately.*

LAIS   Love me!

TELOC   No, I don't love you. You are alone and abandoned. You are no longer the helpless little girl who would run out of the orphanage; today you are the center of a show and your concessions.

LAIS   I earned it.

TELOC   Look at my hand. I send you a thousand images of confusion.

LAIS   Listen, we can leave everything behind. Come with me. We can quit all this together. We'll take a boat and drift in it together. I'll sit up front and you'll stay in the center with your sun hat. You'll work the movie projector. See how I'm rowing.

>   LAIS *rows.* TELOC *puts on his hat and works a projector which is placed on a tripod.*

TELOC   Don't row so hard, you'll knock me over.

LAIS   Look, the film is projected on a screen formed by the mist on the lake.

TELOC   Be careful, you chose the route where the giant octopus congregate: they could reach in with their thousands of tentacles and grab us and pull us down into the black depths.

LAIS   Now I can see the film . . . it's the story of a shepherd girl who loves insects.

TELOC   Those are not insects.

LAIS   Oh, that's right, they're robots. Look, lying next to her is a sleeping harvest reaper in his overalls, and in his dream he sees the shepherdess naked as a statue.

TELOC   But behind her looms the shadow of death!

LAIS   I love you, Teloc.

>   They drop the "boat," the "projector," and the "oars."

TELOC   Lais!

LAIS   Put a string around my neck and I'll be your

trained flea, or put a spiked collar on me and I'll be your watchdog and protect you.

TELOC   Don't touch me.

LAIS   Oh yes, just like when I was at the orphanage. I can't touch you. I can't touch you. I know that I'm not worthy of you. But if you'd like, I'll be your humble giraffe and I'll spend the day stretched out the window so that I can tell you when the clouds form a memory and months of January.

TELOC   Did you remember me?

LAIS   I've looked for you all these years.

TELOC   You were a recluse.

LAIS   That didn't matter . . .

TELOC   Did you travel too?

LAIS   No . . . but take me anywhere you like . . . even back to those times when they persecuted me.

Lighting changes. LAIS *is stretched across a standing torture block.* TELOC *puts on a hood.*

LAIS   What do you want of me? I haven't done anything. I can't remember having done anything.

TELOC (*violently*)   Try, you'll remember!

LAIS   I don't know what this is all about. I'm just a poor young woman in a strange place. All I want is to be free.

TELOC   What do you mean by that?

LAIS   I'm not a witch, nor an enchantress. I haven't done anything wrong.

TELOC   Remember what you did!

LAIS   I swear to you that I've . . .

TELOC   By whom do you swear, hypocrite? By God or by the Devil?

LAIS   Why do you abuse me, what have I done?

TELOC   You're saying that we abuse you?

LAIS   I didn't mean to say . . .

TELOC   Because we arrested and imprisoned you there must be a reason, it's up to you to admit it.

LAIS   I swear I don't know why, I don't!

TELOC   That makes things all the worse. What you are clearly saying, in your sneaky way, is that we have arrested you without any motive. In other words, your presence here is proof of our "injustice," which means that our tribunal is not guided by the unique desire to discover the truth.

LAIS   No, no, I didn't want to say anything like that. You don't understand, I just . . .

TELOC   (*changing his tone suddenly*)   You are our friend, consider us as yours, open your heart, tell us everything. We are all men of honor, we keep our word. Have confidence in us.

LAIS   I'm glad to hear that. Untie me so that I may speak more comfortably.

TELOC   I cannot do that, my girl. I don't give the orders around here. I'm here to help you to seek clemency of those who will dispose of you. Speak to me as you are. Tell me what you have done and why you have perhaps committed blasphemy against us . . . if by chance that is the reason you were arrested?

LAIS   But I did no such thing, I assure you. What makes you think . . . ?

TELOC   (*angrily*)   Well then, since you did not commit blasphemy, you must have done something much worse.

LAIS   Never! But look, without free will how can there

be love, and if you punish me for blasphemy, how can you reward love?

TELOC   Then you admit you committed blasphemy!

LAIS   No, I admit nothing. All I'm saying is that God preaches love and forgiveness and not accusation and punishment, and yet in the name of God you . . .

TELOC   You speak words of the Devil. There is proof enough of your blasphemy. Not satisfied with insulting God, you wish also to condemn our religion and those of us who are its humble servants! You are a monster of arrogance!

LAIS   No, I repeat, I never committed blasphemy, I never committed blasphemy, I only want to make you understand . . .

TELOC   Prideful wench! Insinuating serpent!

LAIS   I beg you, I'm just a simple woman, a human of no importance, I didn't want to irritate you. Please know that I am not a monster of pride or arrogance because I'm afraid, I'm terribly afraid, and thinking of my punishment fills me with terror.

TELOC   So now you're afraid! But when it comes to insulting God, deprecating God, are you afraid then?

LAIS   How can one insult God? How can a simple mortal insult or hurt the Creator?

TELOC   You speak the words of the Devil, I say. Confess to what you have done!

LAIS   I cannot know what I have done. How can I guess why you have arrested me?

TELOC   (*furious*) Guards! Take her to the underground cells and no one is to know where she is.

The action continues "normally."

LAIS   Come live with me.

TELOC *shakes his head "no."*

Do what you want with me.

TELOC *shakes his head again.*

Love me.

TELOC *shakes his head again.*

Then let me love you!

TELOC   May I decapitate you?

LAIS   Oh yes, yes, you may! Look, I'll lay myself down
on this table and you may plunge a dagger into my
breast, tear off strips of my flesh, then pour boiling
wax into the open wounds.

TELOC   I'll do nothing.

LAIS   Drill a hole in my skull and suck out my brains
with a straw.

TELOC   You used to ask me for this sort of thing when
you were a little girl.

LAIS   Yes, yes, make me suffer.

TELOC   I can't.

LAIS   I'll give up the theater, I'll leave everything
behind.

TELOC   You want us to live together?

LAIS   Oh yes.

TELOC   Look at my heart.

*Projections on the columns of the following im-
ages accompanied by a tic-tac beating: Photo of a*

crowd. An insane man in an asylum. Cartoon strips. "The Schoolchildren" by Breughel. A train. "Spring" by Botticelli.

LAIS I love you!

She runs all around the stage, climbs to the top of one of the columns, hangs there by her feet, head hanging down. Her face brushes against TELOC's. *They kiss.* LAIS *comes down and chases after* TELOC. *She catches him and brings him to stage center, making him cross his arms on his chest in a somewhat solemn attitude. She drapes a cape with baroque ornaments about his shoulders, curtsying continuously as she does this. We see an image of what looks like a Boy Scout in dress uniform standing at attention. A serpent wraps itself around him.* LAIS *puts on a horse's harness and gives the reins to* TELOC.

My Lord, your humble servant is not worthy of uniting herself with you for eternity. Order me to wash your feet and I'll dry them with my hair, order me to bring you drink and I shall carry the receptacle on my head to you, order me to write and I shall open my veins so that you may therein dip your pen.

TELOC Have the vehicle and the will power brought to me.

TELOC *climbs into a sort of cart (with rubber wheels) that* LAIS *brings to him. She attaches herself to it as though she were a horse. She pro-*

ceeds to pull the cart with TELOC *in it.* TELOC
guides her with the reins. Suddenly LAIS *stops and
leaves the cart as she takes off the harness.*

LAIS   Kiss me.

They kiss.

When you begin to feel weak, I shall rock you.

TELOC   You know that every night I take out my
compass and measure the distance between two
stars.

LAIS   I'll measure it with you.

TELOC   And now prepare me a stew with a lot of lard
and onions in it. That's the way I like it.

LAIS   Oh yes, I'll make it just the way you like it.

TELOC   We'll dine together.

LAIS   We'll eat with our fingers.

TELOC   Yes, we'll even eat the sauce that way and let
the grease roll down the corners of our mouths . . .

LAIS   Did you know that was a dream I always had
when I was small: having a husband for whom I'd
cook rich, heavy food.

TELOC   And we'll bathe ourselves on the terrace and
over our naked bodies we'll pour noodle soup, and
sardines in oil, and pineapple syrup, and an ointment
called pride.

LAIS   You'll accept me?

TELOC   Come!

LAIS   I'm so lucky!

TELOC   Come!

LAIS   Will you caress me before we go to sleep?

TELOC   Come!

LAIS   Will you squeeze my ass in your big hands too,
but without really hurting me a lot, just a little?
Will you?

TELOC   With the tips of my fingers.

LAIS   And when we go to bed I'll say that I don't want
to undress and you'll play along saying "don't you
feel well?" or "does your back hurt?" and you'll be
the doctor and undress me slowly, or roughly, like
a drunkard, until I'm naked in front of you.

TELOC *points to the balcony and whistles.*

TELOC (*calls out*)   Come up!

LAIS   What's going on?

TELOC   Nothing!

LAIS   Who are you calling?

TELOC   My companion.

LAIS   You live with someone?

TELOC   Of course!

LAIS *climbs to the top of a column and remains
there crouched, silent.*

TELOC   You're not saying anything. Are you angry?

LAIS *turns, remains silent.*

LAIS (*very sadly*)   That jam jar carries my soul. Look,
there it is. Lais' soul dangles in the jam jar at the
end of a ribbon.

TELOC   You kept it. It's the jar I gave you.

LAIS   I've made so many wishes on the jar.

TELOC   For example.

LAIS   Not to die of starvation nor of thirst.

TELOC   And no one has touched it?

LAIS   No one!

TELOC   But you don't believe in its power.

LAIS   It was a souvenir of you.

TELOC   Are you sad?

LAIS   I'll stay alone with the jar and you will go back to your . . .

TELOC   You don't really believe that your soul is in the jar. Can I put my finger in there?

LAIS   No, don't . . . well, I guess if you want to . . .

TELOC   Look! I take it. I remove the cover, do you feel anything?

LAIS   (*feeling pleasure*)   I feel as though a breath of fresh air has blown into my head and my life. My neck and my brain are being brushed by a thousand petals as though a thousand tiny flies without wings had just landed.

TELOC   I'm sticking my finger in.

LAIS   No!

TELOC   A little bit?

It looks as though LAIS *is feeling pain.*

Look, my finger gets closer.

LAIS   I feel a terrible pain hovering over my head.

TELOC   My finger's going in.

LAIS   No . . . oh, do it if it gives you pleasure.

TELOC *closes the jar.*

TELOC   Yes, your soul really is in there, isn't it?

LAIS   Take it. It's yours, keep it. Spread my soul on a piece of toast and if it isn't sweet enough I'll give you some honey to put on it.

There is a knock at the door.

TELOC   Open up, it's her.
LAIS   Who?
TELOC   Her.

> LAIS *opens the door.* MIHARCA *appears dressed in a grotesque outfit. A flood of light bathes her. A toy truck passes at great speed from stage left to right; chasing it is a midget. A drum introduction is heard. A moment of hysteria. The following images project on the wall at great speed: A rayfish. Multicolors. A giant eye. Multicolors. "La Pierre et la Folie" of Bosch.* MIHARCA *appears to be a madwoman with wild, uncontrolled gestures. She laughs hysterically upon seeing* LAIS. *Then she leaps about with great bounds. Finally she throws herself at* LAIS' *feet.*

MIHARCA   Lais . . . (*In a half mocking tone.*) . . . my sweet, my frail and faithful angel.
LAIS   Miharca!
MIHARCA   Prayer for the refrigerator. . . . Dear Father . . .
LAIS   Miharca, you remember?
MIHARCA   Don't pay any attention to me, dear Lais, heart of my heart!

> *All of a sudden,* MIHARCA *starts running about the stage wildly. During this time,* TELOC *has taken a place in a kind of armchair throne. He seems absent, and suddenly very old; he doesn't seem to be aware of what is taking place around him.*

MIHARCA   Watch out for him, he's crazy. Completely crazy. He is a very dangerous man. I'm warning you out of friendship, out of love for you; he's a raving maniac. (*She is frantic, gesticulating wildly.*)

LAIS   He can hear us.

MIHARCA (*screaming*)   Ha! Not a word, the poor man is half deaf. (*Very softly.*) Isn't that right, darling, that you are half deaf?

TELOC (*impassive in his armchair*)   Yes, that's right, dear.

MIHARCA   It's so wonderful . . . who would have thought that he and I . . . it always seemed like it would be you two who would make it.

LAIS   Has it been long since you and he . . .

MIHARCA   Tell me confidentially, Lais, I'm your friend after all, do you really like him?

LAIS *is about to answer, but* MIHARCA *interrupts her.*

Because if you do, if you find him seductive, even if it's only physically, I'll gladly give him up to you. What do you say?

LAIS *is about to answer.* MIHARCA *interrupts again.*

Don't say anything. I know you're aware of what he's become, an impotent, half-paralyzed creature who can't utter a word. He looks as though he could speak, but he's really asleep. Come, you'll see. (MIHARCA, *with gestures of a madwoman, goes to* TELOC.) Yoo-hoo! Go ahead and spit on him, you'll see he won't say anything.

65

TELOC *remains seated, immobile.*

LAIS   Leave him alone, please.

MIHARCA   Spit on him, I said. He loves it. Give him a kick in his parts, go ahead . . . (*She laughs her mad laugh.*) He doesn't even know what's going on.

LAIS   Either he doesn't know or he's enjoying it.

MIHARCA   Aren't you clever! You haven't changed a lick, have you? So intelligent, you always were the first to catch on to things. That's the reason you've been a success in life and the rest of us have failed.

LAIS   Me, a success?

MIHARCA   Of course, come now, don't play modest. You've been a success because you deserve it, you're sensitive and clever, while he and I, we're just a couple of asses.

> MIHARCA *embraces* TELOC *in a vulgar manner and covers his face with kisses. She runs her hands over his body.* TELOC *remains impassive, as though unaware of anything.*

Kiss me, my lover, kiss me. See how Lais watches us. See how she mocks us. Kiss me so we can show her we at least know how to kiss.

LAIS   What are you saying?

MIHARCA   Oh stop the kidding, I know very well that you have only contempt for us. I know it, and furthermore we deserve it.

LAIS   Don't say that. I have no contempt for you, on the contrary.

MIHARCA   Did you hear that, my love?

She runs wildly to TELOC, *feels him up, she is lustful and mad.*

She's sincere, she wants to show us she has real affection for us, she wants to help us. Don't take offense, she didn't mean to insult you. You understand, don't you?

TELOC *clacks his tongue.*

My poor darling, my poor sweet thing! (*She hugs* TELOC's *head to her breast, lovingly, almost maternally.*) He's like a child, he needs loving care. He's amusing and sensitive, like a child. I beg you, please don't do anything that might offend him. You promise, don't you?

LAIS But Miharca . . .

MIHARCA Don't say anything, I understand. Here, come close. It's a secret. Look, he's half-asleep . . . but his eyes are open, he hears, understands, sees nothing.

LAIS I see.

MIHARCA Listen, put your ear next to his heart, you'll hear what a strange noise it makes.

LAIS No, leave me alone . . .

MIHARCA Do it!

MIHARCA *forces* LAIS *to do it. We hear the terrifying noise of a locomotive.* LAIS *pulls back, frightened.* MIHARCA *laughs wildly.*

Did you hear that? You almost went deaf, right? Isn't he funny? You wouldn't think it looking at him, he looks so calm.

LAIS   Leave him alone.

MIHARCA   Look, you want to see how marvelous and different he is. Raise his eyelids and look. (*She does it. She touches* TELOC *and examines him as though he were an inanimate object.*) Raise them yourself.

LAIS *refuses.*

Oh go ahead, do it. And pull out his lips too, and look at his mouth.

LAIS *finally does it.* TELOC *lets out a scream.*

MIHARCA (*to* TELOC)   Oh now, don't be upset dear. She was a bit rough and it hurt a little, but there's no reason . . . oh look, she's made you bleed, my poor sweet.

LAIS   But I didn't mean to.

MIHARCA   Oh I know, don't bother making excuses. You pulled too hard and you made him bleed, that's all there is to it. It's not that terrible. He knows you didn't mean any harm, it was just clumsiness. (MIHARCA *whispers into* TELOC's *ear loudly.*) You see how she is, she made you bleed. You see how she treats us, she did it deliberately.

LAIS   Can't I do something?

MIHARCA   Don't worry about it. Actually, he loves it. He often asks me to beat him. Look! (*She takes a belt and strikes him a hard blow.*) Did you see his face? He loves it. He adores it.

She runs wildly around the stage and finally sits down in a corner and sobs. Her hysteria takes over.

LAIS *goes to her.* MIHARCA *calms down and seems to speak reasonably.*

Lais, I'm sorry about all this, I don't know what came over me.

LAIS   Miharca, I don't understand . . .

MIHARCA   Lais, I'm a hysteric, I know it.

LAIS   We all get hysterical.

MIHARCA   Speak to me, tell me about yourself, I'm so miserable.

LAIS   It's you who should speak, it's been so long since we've seen each other.

MIHARCA   We learned about your success, your triumphs, and we were so happy . . .

LAIS   Why didn't you come before?

MIHARCA   We belong to your childhood. You were living the adventure of your adult life.

LAIS   If you only knew how much I wanted to find you.

MIHARCA   Do you still remember your childhood, the orphanage, the sisters? You must have had such extraordinary experiences since then.

LAIS   My childhood is more with me now than ever, and my adolescence!

MIHARCA   Do you still remember the day you were locked in the cell and the sisters had taken your clothes off so you wouldn't run away, and I stole a big bathrobe for you so you could escape anyway? Remember how we laughed at the way you looked in that huge bathrobe?

LAIS   How did it happen that Teloc . . .

MIHARCA   Teloc was yours then, remember?

LAIS   I feel like I'm dreaming. I have the feeling that something is guiding me toward my destiny, I don't know what or who.

MIHARCA, *crying.*

What is it, Miharca?

MIHARCA   Oh Lais, I want you to be more and more successful, and that you go from triumph to triumph until you enter the garden of delights. What can I do for you? I'll do anything, and so will Teloc.

LAIS   But . . .

MIHARCA   I'm sure your triumph and happiness can only be guaranteed by some sacrifice, and if you wish, I'm ready to make it.

LAIS   What an idea! I won't hear of it.

MIHARCA   You know, when we were little I thought only of you. Let me kiss your hands.

LAIS *puts out her hands.* MIHARCA *kisses them.*

I wish I were a soldier, an officer, so you would look at me differently.

LAIS   Look at you differently?

MIHARCA   As though I weren't a . . .

LAIS   A what?

MIHARCA   Kiss me on the mouth!

LAIS   But why?

MIHARCA   Yes, kiss me on the mouth.

LAIS *kisses her lightly on the mouth.*

You see, you do hate me.

LAIS   How can you say that?

MIHARCA   Then kiss me better.

LAIS *does so unwillingly. Long kiss.* LAIS *pulls abruptly away with a little cry.* MIHARCA *laughs.*

LAIS You bit me!

> MIHARCA *laughs wildly. At that moment* TELOC *approaches, "transformed."*

TELOC That's very good, children, very good. Well now, let's see what else you know how to do. (*He takes a whip and snaps it in the air.*) All right, let's hear you whinny, loud and clear.

> MIHARCA *whinnies.* LAIS *remains mute and doesn't move.* TELOC *becomes furious.*

What now, you won't whinny? Grab her.

> MIHARCA *grabs* LAIS *by the hands and* TELOC *hits her with the whip. Angrily.*

And the next time, it'll really hurt. (*He sounds like an animal trainer.*) All right, my little mares, whinny together.

> *He snaps his whip and they whinny together.*

There now, that's much better. And now I want to see you trot about like a pair of mares. Go on.

> *He snaps his whip. They break into a little trot and whinny.*

Perfect! Now kiss the soles of my boots.

> MIHARCA *rushes to obey the order.* TELOC *points to* LAIS.

She's being difficult again. Hold her!

Before MIHARCA *has a chance to move,* LAIS *quickly kisses the boots.*

Perfect, that's much better.

Circus music is heard and the two women trot and whinny about the stage.

Now it gets a bit more difficult. I want you to go through the hoop of flames. (TELOC *spins a flaming hoop.*)

MIHARCA *and* LAIS *go through it. Fireworks. Projection of following images: Inquisition. Bosch. Cartoon strips. Garden of Delights.*

Darkness. MIHARCA *and* LAIS, *as young girls. Hangman's shadow looms across the stage.*

MIHARCA (*young girl*)   Poor little Lais, always being punished.

LAIS (*young gir*l)   I'm very hungry and cold.

MIHARCA   How long have you been in the cell now?

LAIS   Four days.

MIHARCA   Poor little Lais. Speak lower, they might hear us.

LAIS   At night they bring me a plate of string beans and I ask the guardian to leave the plate and not take it away once I've finished the way she's supposed to do. So I let the beans sit there in their juice until they become all swollen and it seems like I'm eating much more that way.

MIHARCA   But you're not abandoned, I'm still here with you.

LAIS   There are rats here with me too.

MIHARCA   But I'm here.

>*Violins. Cannon shots. Darkness. Dim lights come up. Between the columns appear the heads of the* SHEEP. *Bleating of* SHEEP. *A sheep's head seems to be laughing out loud.* MIHARCA *and* LAIS *as young girls appear on stage.*

LAIS   Come quickly, take all my picture cutouts and give them to all my friends. I'm going to die.

MIHARCA   Don't say that.

LAIS   Yes, yes, I'm going to die and since I've done bad things, I'm going to die a sinner.

MIHARCA   No, you're not going to die. Whatever gave you such an idea suddenly? How could you die at thirteen years of age?

LAIS   Miharca, I know I'm dying. And I haven't done one good deed. I haven't obeyed one rule this month and I took a bath without my nightdress on and oh, I looked at my body and everything.

MIHARCA   But God will forgive that.

LAIS   Sister told me that that was a very big sin.

MIHARCA   Don't worry about it. I know, put on the string of thorns.

LAIS   If I wear that will God forgive me?

MIHARCA   I'm sure of it.

LAIS   I don't have one here.

MIHARCA   I'll give you the one sister gave me for Christmas. It's for the waist and you have to tie it real tight til the thorns stick in your flesh.

LAIS   And God will forgive me?

MIHARCA   It's guaranteed.

LAIS   But I've done nothing but commit sins. I touched my face, and my body, its awful.

MIHARCA   Poor little Lais.

LAIS   And then I never wear the wraparound to flatten my breasts.

MIHARCA   There's still hope.

LAIS   No, I'm going to die . . . you'll bury me in the church crypt right here on the orphanage grounds.

MIHARCA   Why are you so hard on yourself? I'll tell you a secret: I happen to know that God loves me very much and I'm going to ask him to let you live.

LAIS   How do you know that God loves you?

MIHARCA   (*glancing about surreptitiously*)   Moses appeared before me while I was praying.

LAIS   Moses, really?

MIHARCA   Yes, Moses. And he spoke to me.

LAIS   What did he say?

MIHARCA   That I was very dear to him, that I should do everything the sisters ask: going to recreation in groups of three instead of groups of two, not to wash my teeth before Communion, never to speak to men who are all dirty . . .

LAIS   What luck to be able to speak to Moses, with his long beard . . .

MIHARCA   You'll see, I'll ask for your life to be spared and it will.

LAIS   But it's too late, there's nothing he can do now. I'm already dying. Please take my cutouts and give them to my friends.

MIHARCA   And how do you know you're already dying?

LAIS   Because blood is running down the inside of my legs, lots and lots of blood!

Cannon shots. Red lights. SHEEP *bleat, frightened.*
One of them moves forward, laughing. Projec-
tions.

Lights up "normal." Action continues "normally."
MIHARCA *and* LAIS, *adults, are kissing. They caress*
each other. Long silence.

TELOC   That's it, a little more.

> *They continue to kiss.* TELOC *snaps his whip in the*
> *air.*

Enough. That's enough!

> *They caress and embrace.*

Did she bite you?

> *Silence.*

I asked you, Lais, did she bite you? If she did, tell
me, and I'll punish her.
LAIS   No, she didn't bite me.
TELOC   Very good, touch her face then. Lais, caress
her face with love.

> LAIS *obeys.*

Get closer to her, put your forehead to her knees.
That's right, now say something romantic.
LAIS *(feigning)*   Miharca . . . the clouds . . . the
knives . . .

TELOC *snaps his whip with impatience.*

MIHARCA (*sincerely*)　Lais, my love . . .
LAIS (*on the verge of tears*)　Let's walk together, like
　when we first met.
MIHARCA　Speak, Lais.

　　　LAIS *caresses her face.*

LAIS　When I used to be punished on Sundays and
　had to spend the afternoons facing a tree and they
　wouldn't let me watch the ball game which was
　going on behind my back, you, Miharca, you stayed
　at a nearby tree so I wouldn't feel as though I was
　all alone.

　　　TELOC *seems satisfied with the way things are
　　　going between them.*

MIHARCA　But one day you met Teloc . . . and then
　you started dreaming of other worlds and other
　times and you went travelling in the past and in the
　future and you forgot about me, Lais!
LAIS　If you want you can tie a string around me and
　I'll fly about at your side like a butterfly around a
　chicken.
MIHARCA　Your head appears in a dream as though it
　were cut off, your head is floating on a river.
LAIS　I imagine you nude in a park of flowers with
　your hair flowing and a dove sitting on top of your
　head, while an electric train runs at your feet.
MIHARCA　Break the spell that ties you to Teloc . . .
　he possesses you, you have lost your freedom.

LAIS Speak!

MIHARCA Free yourself of him, tear your feelings for him into a thousand pieces until you're completely free again.

LAIS Miharca!

TELOC *snaps his whip.*

TELOC (*to* MIHARCA) That's enough. Admit why you've come here.

MIHARCA What are you doing?

TELOC The game's over. Tell me why you've come to see Lais after so many years. Tell us both.

MIHARCA Because I wanted to be with her, because I always felt great love for her.

TELOC You liar.

MIHARCA Shut up, Teloc!

TELOC You came here to humiliate her, to infuriate her.

MIHARCA Don't say things like that in front of Lais.

TELOC Why, doesn't she have the right to know the truth?

MIHARCA What truth?

TELOC That you envy her, that you hate her!

MIHARCA *screams hysterically.*

MIHARCA (*lifting her skirt over her hips*) Kiss it, kiss it!

TELOC You've already said that to Lais.

MIHARCA I'm going mad!

TELOC That's right, go mad.

MIHARCA The way you insult me . . . the way you abuse me when she's here!

77

LAIS   I forgive you.

MIHARCA   (*stops her hysterics and says with quiet calm and hatred*)   Who are you to forgive me? Who are you, you phony bit of fluff? You think just because you crawl around a stage jabbering silly words you've got the right to . . .

LAIS   I didn't mean to . . .

TELOC   (*to* LAIS)   You should be furious with her. She's trying to run you down. She came today a few hours before your greatest opening night to jinx you, to make you fail. And everything she ever did in the past was not for your good, but that so you would fail. Even I played with your feelings the way she told me to.

LAIS   It's not possible.

TELOC   You have a right to revenge.

LAIS   No.

TELOC   What do I have to do, show you?

LAIS   Show me what?

MIHARCA   No, don't.

TELOC   Do you remember our trips in time?

LAIS   Yes, yes.

TELOC   I'll take you on another trip: you'll see what's going to take place in two hours.

MIHARCA   No, don't!

Darkness. SHEEP *bleating. Projections.*

Light changes. ZENON *cries out, his cage vacillates from above the stage. He calls down.*

ZENON   Kill . . . kill . . . kill . . .

At stage center is a huge cutting blade fixed to a slab. It is the kind of contraption used for slicing down huge fish. It is a kind of guillotine. MIHARCA *is tied to the slab, her head hangs over the side toward the audience. One touch to the huge blade and she will be sliced in two.*

Kill . . . kill her . . . gouge her eyes . . . kill . . .

MIHARCA *is terrified, screaming.* TELOC *and* LAIS *appear on stage.* TELOC *plays the horse and* LAIS, *the rider. They are laughing uncontrollably, like children playing a wild game. They circle around* MIHARCA, *shouting and screaming laughter.* TELOC *passes over* MIHARCA. *She howls.*

Kill her . . . gouge . . . her eyes.

TELOC *and* LAIS *fall to the floor and roll about together near* MIHARCA, *who continues to howl.*

Gouge out . . . her eyes.

LAIS *climbs onto* TELOC *as a horse and together they trot around the stage.* LAIS *seizes an imaginary "lance" and jabs* MIHARCA. LAIS *and* TELOC *scream with laughter.*

Eyes . . . Eyes!

Bleating of SHEEP. *Moment of silence. We hear only* ZENON's *heavy breathing and the insults* MIHARCA *hurls at* LAIS. TELOC *looks as though he is praying, all crouched into himself.* LAIS *goes to*

*the hanging blade and prepares to release the
mechanism which will cut* MIHARCA *in half.*

MIHARCA   No, no, you bitch, you cheap phony!

LAIS *drops the blade and cuts her in half at the
belly. Light turns bright red.* MIHARCA *dies. A
moan comes from* ZENON *above. Bleating of* SHEEP.
*Cannon shots alternate with sounds of praying
in the darkness, for a long moment. Projections.*

Lights up "normal." The action continues "normally."

LAIS (*to* TELOC)   It's not possible, it's not possible.
TELOC (*to* LAIS)   You saw how the rancorous night
    made off with your loneliness.
LAIS   It's not possible!
TELOC   The future surprises you as it should.
LAIS   Miharca! Miharca!
ZENON's VOICE   Lais!
LAIS   Be still! (*To* TELOC.) Where is Miharca?
TELOC   She has disappeared.

MIHARCA *comes forward from the back of stage
center as though she were a phantom. She speaks
as though sleepwalking.*

MIHARCA   I am the adulterous princess of the serpents.
    Look at my breast.
LAIS (*looking*)   I don't see anything!
MIHARCA   Look at my breast and you will see the
    burning bonze, the naked woman, the vultures, and

if you look more closely you will perceive the futility of life.

LAIS   I see also two children playing with the hoop of my thoughts.

MIHARCA   You will no longer be the virgin nor the Devil.

Suddenly TELOC *pulls out his whip again.*

TELOC   Tell her you hate her!

MIHARCA (*with conviction*)   I hate you!

LAIS   Miharca!

MIHARCA   I hate you with all my gut hate. I hate you as though you were the stillborn child I never desired.

LAIS   Be still, Miharca.

TELOC *snaps his whip.*

Light changes.

TELOC (*as cross-examining lawyer*)   And of what are you accused?

LAIS (*defendant*)   Uh, well . . . but will you agree to defend me during my trial? . . . you have such a good reputation . . . you who are the best lawyer in this area.

TELOC   Well, tell me first what is the crime of which you are accused.

LAIS   I, uh . . .

TELOC (*dignified*)   It seems that you have committed blasphemy.

LAIS   You are a lawyer . . .

TELOC   Yes, I am devoted to justice.

LAIS Well then . . .

TELOC Is there anything more stimulating than a
trial? You speak out to the country directly repre-
sented by the judge, you have the right to tell them
anything you wish, to enter into dialogue with them.

LAIS How I would love for you to defend me.

TELOC My child, I do not wish in the slightest to hurt
your feelings nor give you the impression that your
case does not interest me, but you must understand
that an affair such as yours offends my conscience
to such a degree that I cannot . . . I believe in God!

LAIS But you believe in a God of love?

TELOC Yes, that's quite right.

LAIS Then how can you refuse to defend me, how can
you allow the expression of a God of accusation and
punishment, a God of revenge?

TELOC My girl, you are fortunate enough to appear
before our judges, who are particularly just and
render sentences typified by their dignity and moder-
ation. You have no need of a lawyer.

LAIS But you . . . haven't you defended men accused of rape, of murder, theft, and embezzlement?
Wasn't your conscience offended then?

TELOC Let us drop the subject.

LAIS No, on the contrary, let us go into it.

TELOC Silence, I must go to Communion.

LAIS Eat well!

Lights "normal." The action continues "normally."
TELOC *finishes the installation of a kind of platform,
stage center, which is covered with a cloth.*

TELOC You want to know everything?

LAIS   Go ahead!

TELOC   Miharca asked me to perform all the "roles" I played with you. She wanted to infuriate you, to show you that you're nothing and a nobody. That your only reality is the world of your childhood and that your success and celebrity today are nothing but lies and illusions.

LAIS   I know that!

TELOC   She made me hurt you.

MIHARCA *lowers the cage and tries to talk to* ZENON. *She throws peanuts at him.*

LAIS   I can't believe it.

TELOC   Her whole attitude seems empty of any meaning, except one. You remember how I was capable of accomplishing all sorts of miracles? Ha! Well, now she has managed to rob me of almost all my faculties. Look at me! Believe me! (*In a stage whisper.*) And I who love only you!

LAIS   Teloc!

TELOC   Be quiet, she will hear us, speak softer.

LAIS   She's busy with Zenon.

TELOC   She is constantly putting me through horrible tortures. Look at my arms. There's nothing left but wounds. Look at my ankles, my legs. You see those collars? They're strings of thorns she makes me wear and which she pulls and tugs on till the thorns dig into my skin and the blood bursts out. She's a monster.

LAIS   Why do you put up with it? . . .

TELOC   I'm at her mercy. She knows my life, she can do what she wants with me. With just a word she can have me locked away for life.

LAIS   Teloc, do you really love me?

TELOC   I'll do anything for you.

LAIS   Let's run away together!

TELOC   Look at her. Now that she knows how attached you are to Zenon, she's plotting to get him away from you . . . she loves only one person in the world . . . you! She is torn between her love and her hate for you!

LAIS   Let's run away.

TELOC   Listen to her.

MIHARCA *playing with* ZENON.

ZENON   You . . . bitch.

MIHARCA   Be still, silly creature.

ZENON   You . . . bitch . . . me . . . and Lais . . .

MIHARCA   Lais is the bitch. Lais locks you up. Look at me, I'm letting you out with this key. I'm setting you free.

ZENON   Lais . . . good.

MIHARCA   I'm letting you out. Lais is bad.

LAIS (*to* TELOC)   Do something.

TELOC (*to* MIHARCA)   You can stop all this, it's over, you're through brutalizing me. You're sick. Lais and I have decided it's time we put a stop to you. Isn't that right, Lais?

LAIS   That's right, yes.

TELOC   You're never going to torture either of us again, and you won't get a chance to turn Zenon against Lais either.

MIHARCA   Shut up, you're more of a monster than Zenon is. She's fed up with him and now she wants to run away with you. She's a conniving bitch and she always has been.

84

TELOC   How can you dare treat Lais like that?

MIHARCA   I'll dare treat her any way I feel like. You revealed all my secrets to her. So now tell her everything, tell her you came to . . .

TELOC   You're the one! You came to destroy her on the day of her greatest triumph!

MIHARCA   No, tell the truth. Tell her I came first to gouge out her eyes, then to kill her.

TELOC   You hate her, you want to kill her, and you prepared this whole scene so that you could enjoy torturing her before killing her.

MIHARCA   That's true, and you were in on the whole thing.

TELOC   Because you made me by threatening me, but now I'm free. (*He grabs her, throws her to the floor, and holds her hands.*) Stuff a handkerchief in her mouth so she can't scream.

LAIS *approaches. She fights with* MIHARCA, *who tries to bite her.*

LAIS   She tried to bite me. She almost ripped my hand off.

TELOC   Watch out for her! Don't get too close, she'll go for your eyes. Take that cloth off there.

LAIS *pulls off the cloth on the platform which reveals the guillotine apparatus with the enormous blade.*

MIHARCA   I'll tear your eyes out!

TELOC   You see how she fights. Your tyranny is finished, you vicious cat, now it's your turn to suffer.

Suddenly, inexplicably, MIHARCA *frees herself, runs toward* LAIS, *and bites her viciously on the ear.*

MIHARCA (*her teeth still clenched in* LAIS' *ear*) If you make one move, Teloc, I'll rip her ear off and then tear out her eyes.

LAIS Please don't do anything Teloc, the pain is terrible.

TELOC Miharca, I beg you, let her go, we'll go away, she won't do anything.

MIHARCA I'll kill you both. You because you're a traitor, and then her.

LAIS Let me go, you're hurting my ear. I can't stand your weight on me.

MIHARCA Well, you'll have to.

TELOC Kill me if you want, but leave her alone.

MIHARCA I'll kill you both and tear out your eyes.

TELOC Look at my string of thorns, I'll tighten them around my flesh if you want.

ZENON *watches the goings on and swings furiously in his cage.*

MIHARCA Go ahead, tighten them, that's good. At the same time I'll break her arm and tear off her ear.

She tears off LAIS' *ear.* LAIS *screams in agony.* LAIS *remains in* MIHARCA's *clutches as she sits on her, pinning her.*

Look, here is her ear, eat it at once, eat it if you want me to let her go. But if you come close, I'll tear out her eyes.

LAIS *moans*.

Bitch!

TELOC (LAIS' *ear in hand*)   If you let her go, I'll eat it, I'll do anything you want.

MIHARCA   You're at my feet now, more than ever before.

TELOC   I'll do anything you like.

MIHARCA   You'll never get away from me.

ZENON *throws a rock at* MIHARCA *from his cage. She falls unconscious.* TELOC *and* LAIS *grab her at once. They beat her brutally, then tie her to the chopping block. After they have finished tying her securely,* MIHARCA *comes to, moaning.*

ZENON (*to* LAIS)   Gouge her . . . eyes . . . gouge . . . eyes!

Cannon shots. Darkness. Projections: Bombs. Planes. Cartoon strips. Goya. Bosch.

The stage looks as it did at the beginning of the Second Act. Telephone rings. LAIS *picks it up. She is alone on stage.*

POLICEMAN'S VOICE   This is the police.

LAIS   Yes.

POLICEMAN'S VOICE   We have solved the Miharca incident; your friend committed suicide. She left a letter in which she said:

MIHARCA'S VOICE   With Teloc's help, I shall offer my life as sacrifice. The hand which will torture and

kill me will be guided by my own voice and wishes,
that way I will celebrate my death with black bottles,
ecstasies, and twining vines.

> LAIS *puts back the receiver. Slowly she walks*
> *around the stage, occasionally kneeling down to*
> *kiss the floor. She sings her song sadly. Numbly,*
> *she kisses the floor again. Bleating of* SHEEP.

LAIS   Zenon, where are the skeletons of my dead sheep,
where have they disappeared?

ZENON   Me . . . love y . . . you.

> LAIS *brings down* ZENON's *cage. At that moment,*
> *the turntable swings around bringing the live*
> SHEEP *into view.*

LAIS   My sweet darlings, how is it possible? My little
ones have been restored to me. (*She kisses them.*)
My darlings, my pretty ones, how I missed you.

ZENON   Me . . . me! Not . . . sheep.

LAIS   Wait a second, be patient. (*She brings down the*
cage entirely.) Zenon, now be good, stay with me
quietly and be good. Come out.

ZENON   Come . . . with m . . . me.

LAIS   Why?

ZENON   Come . . . in . . . egg.

> *They go into the egg through the little door.*

Now . . . throw . . . away . . . k . . . key.

LAIS   Throw away the key? But we'll be imprisoned in
here.

ZENON   Throw . . . key . . . Throw!

LAIS Yes, yes, I'll throw away the key. You are my light and my night and my happiness. But before, Zenon, take this jar of jam. (*She hands him the jar containing her soul.*)

ZENON (*eating with his fingers*) Jam . . . good, good . . .

> *When he has finished eating it, he becomes a "human being" and begins speaking "normally."*

What a delicious taste!

> *They take places in the egg and* LAIS *throws away the key.*

LAIS Ze . . . non . . . m . . . my sheep . . . alive!

ZENON (*speaking perfectly*) The live sheep are yours, they cry for you, you are life and hope for us. I love you desperately!

LAIS Me . . . me . . . love . . . y . . . you, Zenon. (*She speaks the way* ZENON *used to speak.*)

> ZENON *sings* LAIS' *song with no difficulty. The egg mounts and swings softly as he does. At that moment,* TELOC *comes on stage accompanying* ZENON's *song on his trumpet. The egg has risen out of sight. We hear the animal laughter of* LAIS *in the egg while* ZENON *sings clearly and well.* TELOC *stands among the* SHEEP *and plays the melody as the curtain comes down.*